I0869520

PLANET NEPTUNE

By Rosie Rowntree

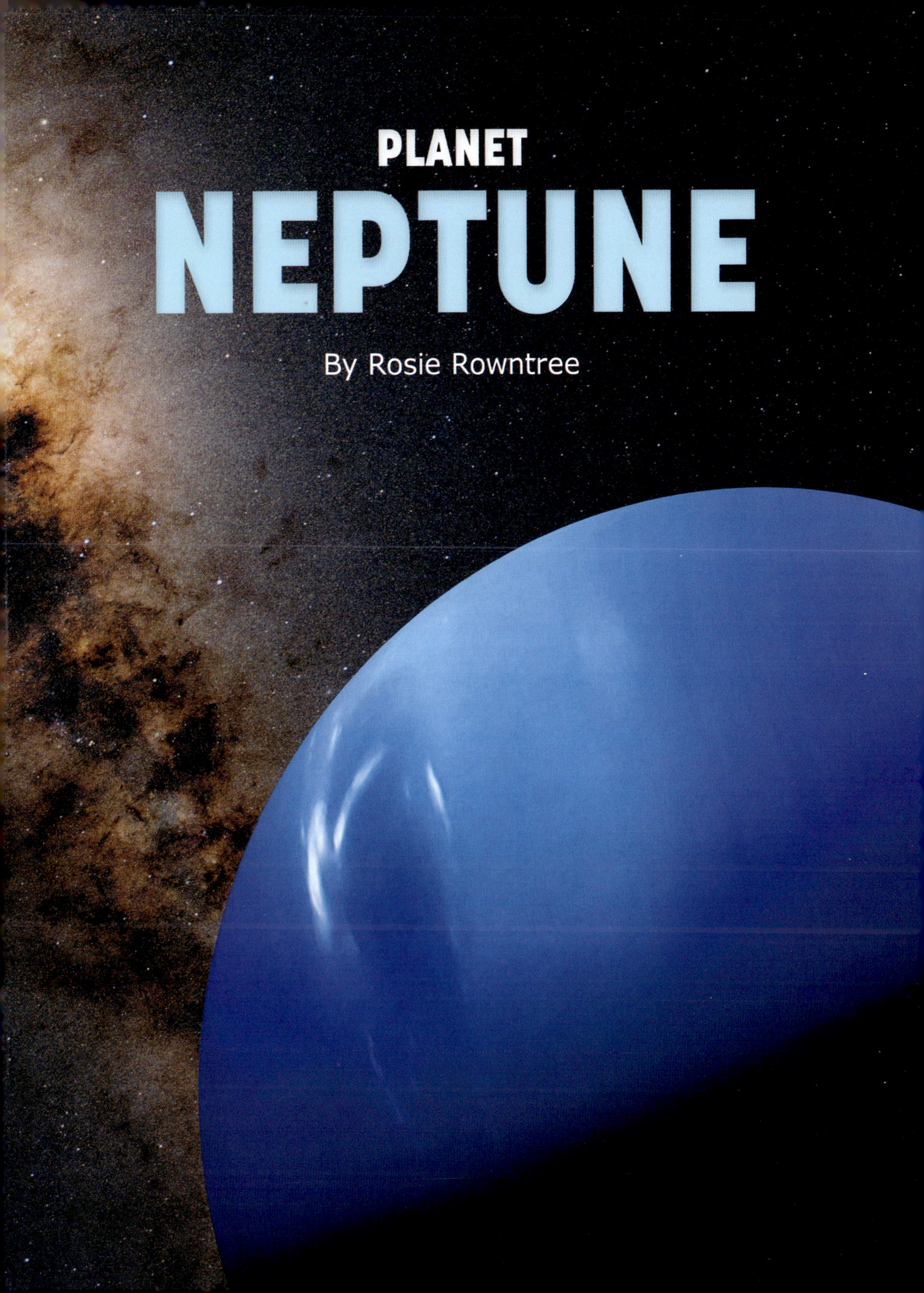

CONTENTS

First published in 2026 by Hungry Tomato Ltd
F15, Old Bakery Studios, Blewetts Wharf, Malpas Road,
Truro, Cornwall, TR1 1QH, UK.

Copyright © 2026 Hungry Tomato Ltd

No part of this publication may be reproduced, stored in a retrieval system, or transmitted in any form or by any means, electronic, mechanical, photocopying, recording, or otherwise, without prior written permission of the copyright owner. A CIP catalog record for this book is available from the British Library.

ISBN 9781835696835

Manufactured in the USA

Discover more at
www.hungrytomato.com

Front cover image is an artist's impression of Neptune as seen from the surface of Triton. Title page image is a edited image of Neptune. Contents page image is an edited image of Neptune.

Words in **BOLD** can be found in the glossary.

WHERE IS NEPTUNE?

There are eight planets in our **solar system**. All of them travel around the Sun. Neptune is the eighth planet from the Sun.

The time it takes a planet to travel around the Sun once is called a year. Neptune travels around the Sun once every 165 **Earth years**! This journey is called Neptune's **orbit**.

PLANET FACTS

Neptune is the fourth biggest planet in the solar system. It is a **gas** planet and doesn't have a solid surface.

Planets are always spinning. The time it takes a planet to spin around once is called a day. One day on Neptune is the same as 16 hours on Earth.

Neptune is an "ice giant" made of a mixture of water and gases. One of these gases, called **methane,** is why Neptune is blue!

Neptune

Pluto

Neptune is the furthest planet from the Sun – sometimes it is even further away than **dwarf planet** Pluto, thanks to Pluto's oval-shaped orbit!

WHAT'S THE WEATHER LIKE?

Neptune is the windiest planet in the solar system! Winds roar around the planet five times faster than they do on Earth.

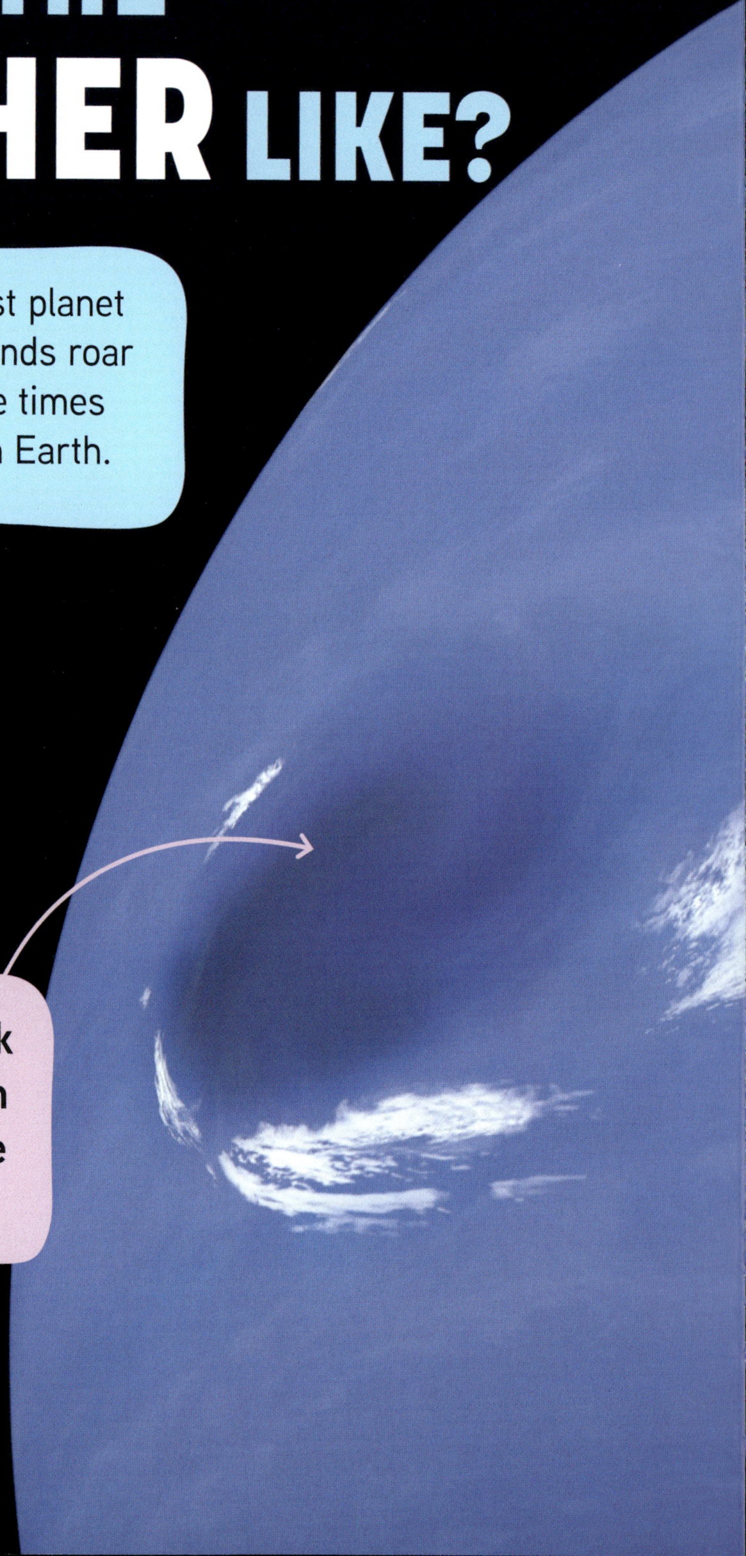

Neptune's Great Dark Spot is a huge storm that is the same size as Earth!

Neptune is also very cold. Temperatures can be as low as -353 °F (-214 °C). The coldest temperature ever recorded on Earth was only -128 °F (-89 °C)!

Several other large storms have also been spotted elsewhere on Neptune.

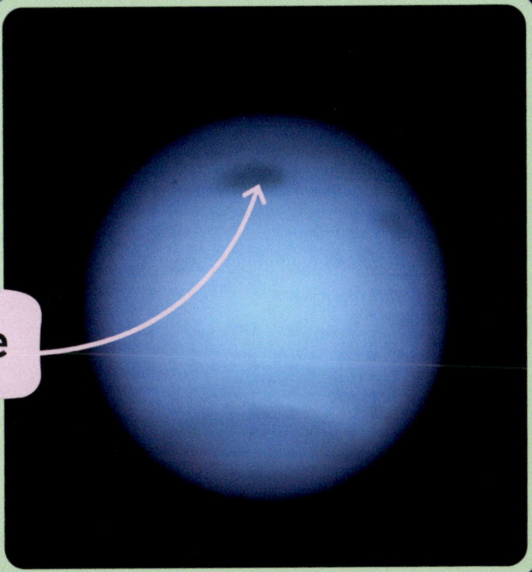

Storm on Neptune

NEPTUNE'S MOONS

Neptune has 16 **moons** that scientists know of. Two of them don't have permanent names yet!

One of the moons that does have a name is Nereid. It is very, very far away from Neptune and takes 360 **Earth days** to complete its unusual oval-shaped orbit!

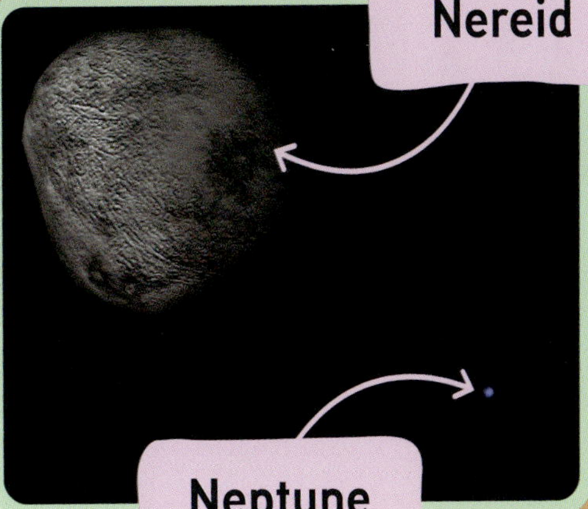

Hippocamp, on the other hand, takes less than one Earth day. It is the smallest of Neptune's moons and is over 100 times smaller than Earth's own Moon!

TRITON

Neptune's largest moon is called Triton. Triton is even colder than Neptune itself and is one of the coldest places in the whole solar system!

The temperature on the surface of Triton can get as low as -391 °F (-235 °C)!

It is so cold that some of the gases in its **atmosphere** have turned into frost, making the surface icy.

Triton also has **geysers** that shoot cold gas and dust up into space!

NEPTUNE'S RINGS

Neptune is surrounded by five rings that are made of chunks of rocks and dust.

Scientists think that these rings were created by some of Neptune's moons crashing into each other, and bits of dust and rocks breaking off.

Neptune's **gravity** then caused these small pieces to stick together, eventually creating the rings.

WHAT CAN WE SEE?

Because Neptune is so far from Earth, it can't be seen with the human eye. You have to use a **telescope**.

Neptune was discovered because **astronomers** noticed that Uranus's orbit around the Sun was a bit strange. They thought that the gravity of a mysterious planet had to be affecting Uranus. That planet turned out to be Neptune!

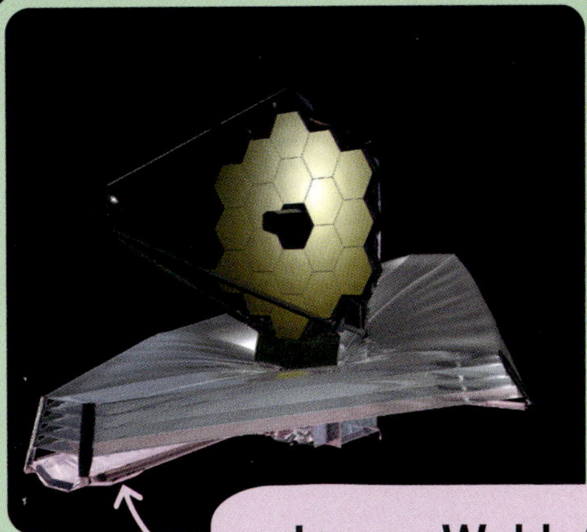

In the present day, **space telescopes** like the **James Webb Space Telescope** can take clear pictures of Neptune. These images help scientists and astronomers study the planet.

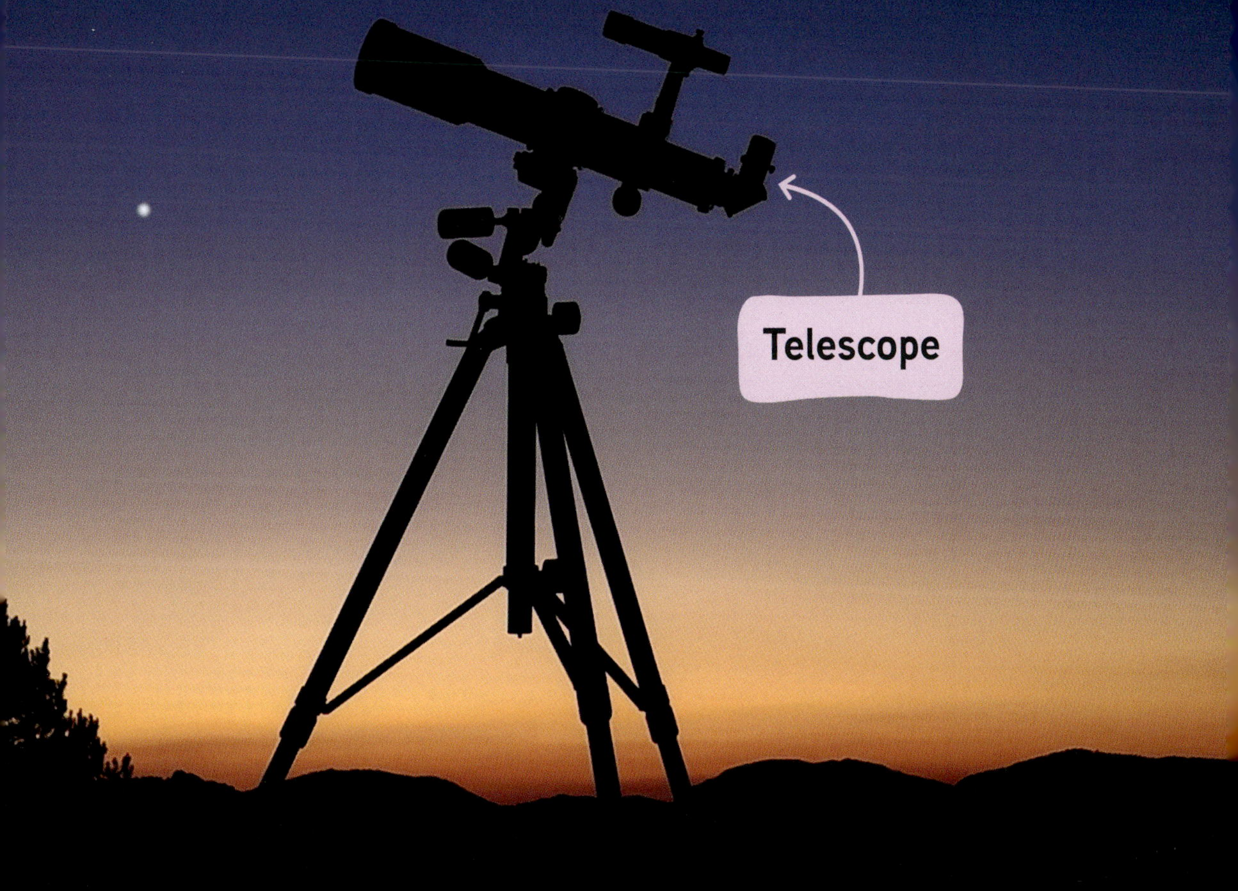

FACT FILE

Like Earth, Neptune has **seasons**. But because Neptune takes so long to orbit the Sun, each season lasts 40 Earth years.

Because of its distance from the Sun, Neptune doesn't get much light. In fact, sunlight on Earth is 900 times brighter than it is on Neptune!

Since its discovery in 1846, Neptune has only completed one orbit around the Sun. It won't finish its next one until the year 2176!

EXPLORING NEPTUNE

Neptune is so far away that only one spacecraft has ever been there!

Voyager 2 made a **flyby** of Neptune on a huge journey around the solar system. It took 12 years to reach Neptune!

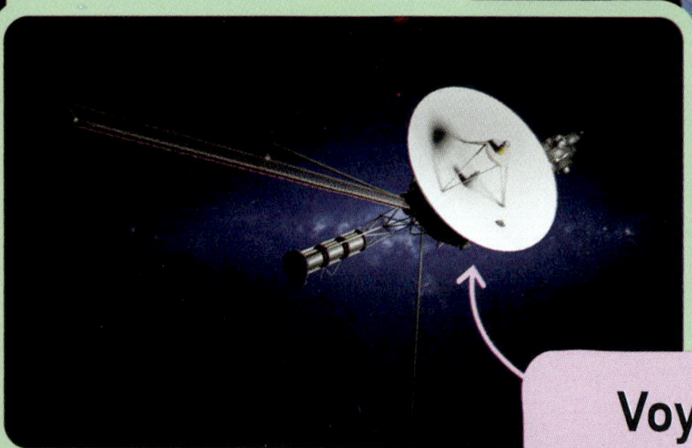

Voyager 2 measured the temperature on Neptune and the speed of its winds.

The spacecraft is now so far away from Earth that it is now in **interstellar space**!

WHAT'S NEXT?

Scientists are eager to explore Neptune and its moons more.

Triton in particular has caught their interest. While the moon itself is billions of years old, its surface is very young. It is being shaped by something – and scientists want to find out what!

Scientists are also wanting to send **probes** to explore Neptune's atmosphere.

Triton is a mix of
rock and ice

GLOSSARY

Atmosphere – the gases that surround a planet or star.

Astronomers – scientists who study space.

Dwarf planet – large, round objects that orbit the Sun, but aren't big enough to be called planets.

Earth days – the amount of time that a day lasts for on Earth (24 hours).

Earth years – the amount of time that a year lasts for on Earth (365 days).

Interstellar space – the space between stars.

James Webb Space Telescope – a telescope in orbit around the Sun.

Flyby – the closest approach of a spacecraft to a planet or moon.

Gas – a substance that is neither solid nor liquid, and has no fixed shape. Many gases are invisible.

Geysers – holes in the ground which hot water, steam, and gases come out of.

Gravity – an invisible force that pulls things together. Gravity keeps our feet on the ground and the planets spinning around the Sun.

Methane – a tasteless gas.

Moons – large, natural objects that orbit a planet.

Orbit – the path taken by one object circling around another in space.

Probes – uncrewed spacecraft sent to explore outer space.

Seasons – different times of the year, with different types of weather. Spring, summer, fall, and winter are all seasons.

Solar system – the Sun and everything that moves around it.

Space telescopes – telescopes in orbit in space.

Telescope – an instrument that makes faraway objects appear bigger.

Picture credits:
(t=top; b=bottom; m=middle; l=left; r=right):

NASA: images-assets.nasa.gov/image/stsci-h-p1904a-m-2000x1143/stsci-h-p1904a-m-2000x1143~orig.jpg 11br. Wikipedia: By NASA, ESA, STScI, M.H. Wong (University of California, Berkeley), and L.A. Sromovsky and P.M. Fry (University of Wisconsin-Madison) - https://www.nasa.gov/feature/goddard/2020/dark-storm-on-neptune-reverses-direction-possibly-shedding-a-fragment, Public Domain 9mr. Unknown: 11tr. Shutterstock: AstroStar 16-17bg; Bryan Vectorartist 14-15bg; Burandaki 6-7bg, 16bl, 18-19bg; Carlosramos1946 7mr; Claudio Caridi 7bl; Elliptic Studio 17tl; Gergitek 18mr; Joshimerbin 21bl; Jurik Peter 12-13bg; ManuMata 20-21bg, 22-23bg; NASA Images 2-3bg; Nemes Laszlo 1bg; Pzykodegoat 8-9bg; Sergey Fedoskin 24bg; Simon Wendler 13br; Triff 4-5bg; Vladim Sadovski 10-11bg.

Every effort has been made to trace the copyright holders, and we apologize in advance for any unintentional omissions. We would be pleased to insert the appropriate acknowledgments in any subsequent edition of this publication.